Holidays

Hanukkah

by Rebecca Pettiford

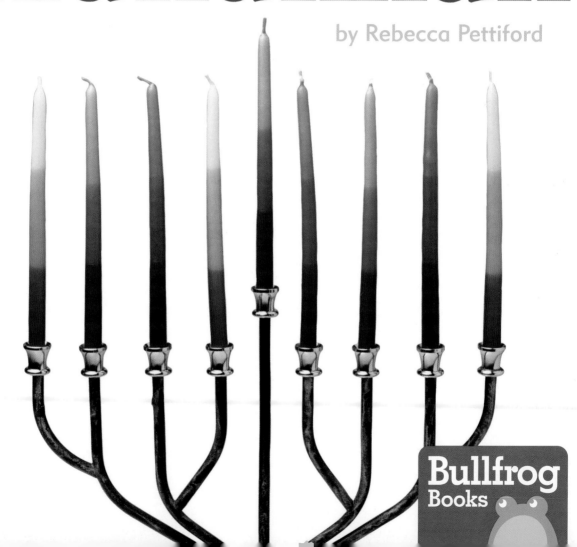

Bullfrog
Books

Ideas for Parents and Teachers

Bullfrog Books let children practice reading informational text at the earliest reading levels. Repetition, familiar words, and photo labels support early readers.

Before Reading

• Discuss the cover photo. What does it tell them?

• Look at the picture glossary together. Read and discuss the words.

Read the Book

• "Walk" through the book and look at the photos. Let the child ask questions. Point out the photo labels.

• Read the book to the child, or have him or her read independently.

After Reading

• Prompt the child to think more. Ask: Does your family celebrate Hanukkah? What sorts of things do you see around Hanukkah?

Bullfrog Books are published by Jump!
5357 Penn Avenue South
Minneapolis, MN 55419
www.jumplibrary.com

Library of Congress Cataloging-in-Publication Data
Pettiford, Rebecca.
Hanukkah / by Rebecca Pettiford.
    pages cm.—(Holidays)
Includes bibliographical references and index.
Summary: "This photo-illustrated book for early readers describes the Jewish holiday of Hanukkah and the things people do to celebrate it."
Provided by publisher.
ISBN 978-1-62031-130-1 (hardcover)
ISBN 978-1-62496-198-4 (ebook)
1. Hanukkah—Juvenile literature. I. Title.
BM695.H3P43 2014
296.4'35—dc23
                                    2013049159

Editor: Wendy Dieker
Series Designer: Ellen Huber
Book Designer: Lindaanne Donohoe
Photo Researcher: Kurtis Kinneman

Photo Credits: All photos by Shutterstock except: Corbis/SuperStock, 6–7; Exactostock/SuperStock, 1, 4, 20–21; Image Asset Management Ltd./SuperStock, 8–9; istock, 12, 16 (inset), 16–17; iStock, cover; Pecold/Shutterstock.com, 23 br; PhotoStock-Israel/Shay Levy/Alamy, 9

Printed in the United States of America at Corporate Graphics in North Mankato, Minnesota.
3-2014
10 9 8 7 6 5 4 3 2 1

Table of Contents

What Is Hanukkah?

Hanukkah is a Jewish holiday.

It is in late fall.

It lasts for eight days.

What do Jews celebrate?

They think about a miracle.

It was a long time ago.

The Jews won a war.

They went to the temple.

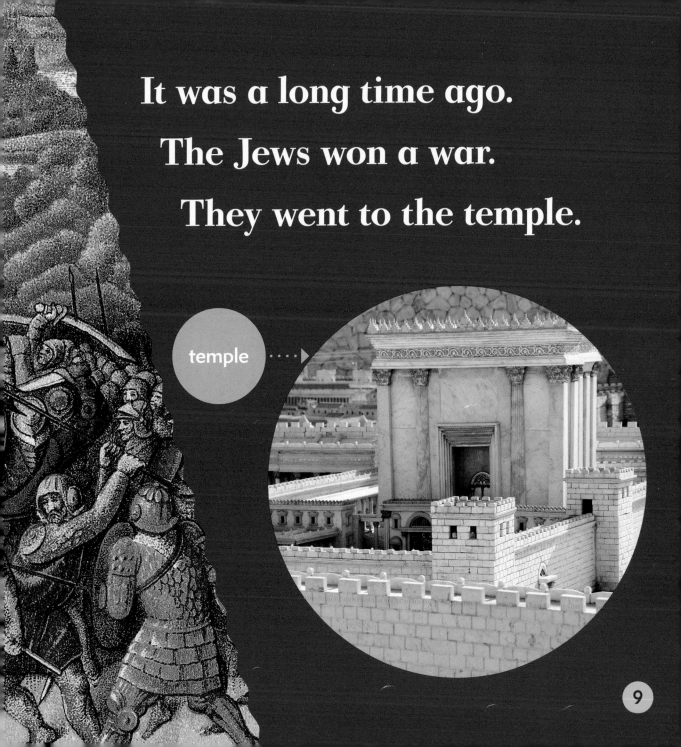

temple ····▶

The men lit an oil lamp.
There was oil for only
one day.

Oh, no!

But it lasted eight days.

Wow!

It is night.

We say a blessing.

Ben lights a candle.

menorah

It sits in a menorah.

latkes

Mom makes latkes.

She uses potatoes.

We eat donuts, too. Yum!

corbis

15

We play a game.

Mira spins a dreidel.

She wins gelt.

Are they coins?

No. Gelt is candy.

gelt

We give gifts.

Leah gets a book.

19

Happy Hanukkah!

Symbols of Hanukkah

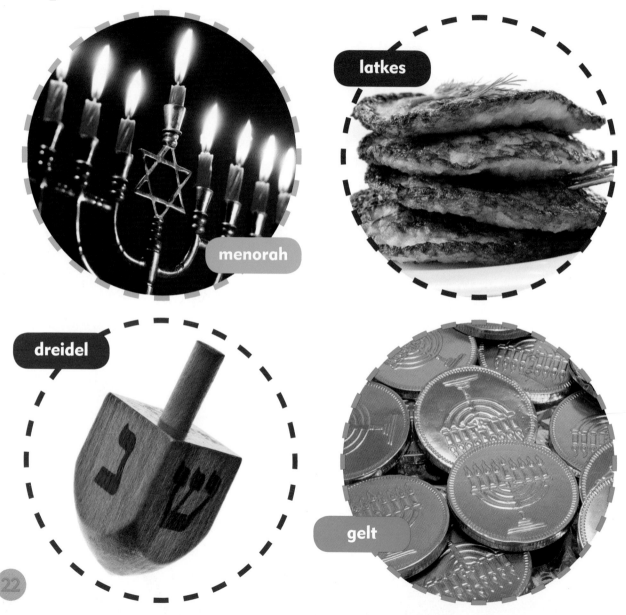

menorah

latkes

dreidel

gelt

Picture Glossary

blessing
A prayer of thanks to God.

oil lamp
A container filled with oil that burns like a candle.

Jew
A person who follows the religion of Judaism and believes in one God.

temple
A place where Jewish people worship.

Index

To Learn More

Learning more is as easy as 1, 2, 3.

1) Go to www.factsurfer.com

2) Enter "Hanukkah" into the search box.

3) Click the "Surf" button to see a list of websites.

With factsurfer.com, finding more information is just a click away.